Little Cakes!

Little Cakes!

25 TINY TASTY TEATIME TREATS

CAROL PASTOR

LORENZ BOOKS

This edition is published by Lorenz Books,
an imprint of Anness Publishing Ltd
108 Great Russell Street, London WC1B 3NA

info@anness.com
www.lorenzbooks.com
www.annesspublishing.com

If you like the images in this book and would
like to investigate using them for publishing,
promotions or advertising, please visit our
website www.practicalpictures.com for
more information.

© Anness Publishing Ltd 2016

A CIP catalogue record for this book is
available from the British Library.

Publisher: Joanna Lorenz
Editor: Helen Sudell
Additional recipes by: Rosie Anness and
  Cortina Butler p36, p38; Anja Hill p50;
  Mowie Kay p60; Hannah Miles p40, p56;
  Ann Nicol p26, p44, p46, p48, p54
Photographers: Nicki Dowey, Craig Robertson,
  William Lingwood
Production Controller: Rosanna Anness

PUBLISHER'S NOTE
Although the advice and information in this
book are believed to be accurate and true at
the time of going to press, neither the authors
nor the publisher can accept any legal
responsibility or liability for any errors or
omissions that may have been made nor for
any inaccuracies nor for any loss, harm or
injury that comes about from following
instructions or advice in this book.

COOK'S NOTES

- Bracketed terms are intended for American readers.

- For all recipes, quantities are given in both metric and imperial measures and, where appropriate, in standard cups and spoons. Follow one set of measures, but not a mixture, because they are not interchangeable.

- Standard spoon and cup measures are level. 1 tsp = 5ml, 1 tbsp = 15ml, 1 cup = 250ml/8fl oz.

- Australian standard tablespoons are 20ml. Australian readers should use 3 tsp in place of 1 tbsp for measuring small quantities.

- American pints are 16fl oz/2 cups. American readers should use 20fl oz/2.5 cups in place of 1 pint when measuring liquids.

- Electric oven temperatures in this book are for conventional ovens. When using a fan oven, the temperature will probably need to be reduced by about 10–20°C/20–40°F. Since ovens vary, you should check with your manufacturer's instruction book for guidance.

- The nutritional analysis given for each recipe, unless otherwise stated, is calculated per portion (i.e. serving or item). The analysis does not include optional ingredients, such as salt added to taste.

- Medium (US large) eggs are used unless otherwise stated.

Contents

Introduction

A sweet treat is a joy to savour, whether it's the finale to a meal, a simple offering to be shared over morning coffee or afternoon tea, a special reward, or a well-earned present. Satisfying to make and gratifying to eat, little cakes and bakes are all about indulgence.

Baking provides so much pleasure There's a real sense of achievement when you create a fresh batch of delicious cakes, and the whole house is filled with the marvellous aroma of baking. Home-made cakes must be the most popular, comforting food you can make, and old favourites are always welcomed, but it's also fun to try something new. This specially selected collection of little sweet bakes offers you the perfect opportunity to create irresistible morsels of delight for family and friends alike.

Above: A cake tier loaded with pretty little cakes makes an original option for a wedding party.

Cakes for all occasions

Little bakes are designed, generally, to be just one or two mouthfuls so that they are easy to eat and your fingers don't get sticky. There are tiny cake pops that are perfect to offer around at a party as sweet canapés; light and fruity muffins, perfect for breakfast; beautifully decorated cupcakes for that special afternoon tea party; and decadent chocolate confections to serve after dinner. The recipes in this book will give you ideas for delicious treats for parties, weddings and year-round celebrations, as well as simpler bakes that are suitable for every day – perhaps for a lunchbox or after-school treat.

Baking skills

Many of these cakes can be made with standard store-cupboard ingredients and none of them are difficult to make. Just a few baking methods are used throughout the book. If you are a less experienced baker, remember that there are no secrets to making delicious cakes, just follow the simple step-by-step methods to ensure successful results. Use the best ingredients

Above: You will need a range of mixing bowls – small, medium and large – for sifting ingredients and mixing.

you can afford to buy. Similarly, choose good quality bakeware and utensils. Always choose the correct tin or pan size, otherwise your cakes may not bake evenly, or according to the times listed for each recipe. Careful weighing and measuring of ingredients is crucial for success, as is using the precise oven temperatures and exact cooking timings. Buy a reliable oven thermometer to test the temperature of your oven if you are unsure of its accuracy.

Before beginning, read the recipe through to ensure you understand every stage. Assemble all of the ingredients to be doubly

Above: Invest in good quality cake tins and pans for perfect results, and always cool cakes on wire racks.

Above: Eggs, sugar, butter and flour are basic ingredients for cake making. Chocolate is a luxury ingredient.

sure that you have them all before you begin, and (unless otherwise stated) for best results allow eggs and butter to come to room temperature before using them.

When possible bake the cakes in the centre of the oven where the heat is more likely to be constant. If you are using a fan-assisted oven, follow the manufacturer's guidelines for baking. Finally, if you are baking more than one item at the same time, swap the positions midway through the baking time to ensure an even distribution of heat. Test to ensure the goods are baked through before removing

them from the oven – they should be golden brown on top and have a 'set' appearance.

Once out of the oven leave the cakes to cool on a wire rack before storing them in an airtight container. Unless otherwise stated in the recipe, most baked goods will taste fresh for up to 3–4 days. You can of course plan ahead and bake and freeze little cakes. Make sure that they are thoroughly defrosted before adding any fillings or decorative toppings.

Tips for successful cake making

Paying attention to the detail of a recipe will help to ensure perfect cakes every time. Gather together all your equipment and prepare your cake tins or pans. Take care with accurate measuring, and know how to test that the cake is cooked so your efforts are rewarded.

Measuring ingredients

If you are trying a new recipe for the first time it is best to follow the instructions carefully. Measuring ingredients precisely will ensure consistent results. Always use the best quality ingredients that are well within their 'use-by' date.

For liquids measured in pints or litres, use a glass or clear plastic measuring jug or cup. For liquids measured in spoons, pour the

Above: Place the measuring jug on a flat surface. Check that the liquid is level with the marking specified in the recipe.

liquid into the measuring spoon, to the brim, and then pour it into the mixing bowl. Do not measure it over the mixing bowl in case of spillages.

For measuring dry ingredients by weight, scoop or pour on to the scales, watching the dial and reading carefully. Balance scales give more accurate readings than spring scales. For measuring dry ingredients in a spoon, fill the spoon, scooping up the ingredients. Level the surface with the straight edge of a knife.

For measuring butter, cut with a sharp knife and weigh, or cut off the specified amount following the markings on the wrapping paper.

To measure syrup, set the mixing bowl on the scales and turn the gauge to zero, or make a note of the weight. Pour in the required weight of syrup.

Melting chocolate

Melting chocolate needs care and attention. Break the bar into small pieces and put it in a heatproof bowl standing over a pan of warm water. Make sure the bowl is dry and that steam cannot get into it. Heat the water to a gentle simmer and leave the bowl to stand for about 5 minutes. Do not let the water get too hot or the chocolate will reach too high a temperature and will lose its sheen.

Preparing tins and pans

When recipes give instructions on how to prepare and line tins, don't be tempted to skip this, or you may ruin your cakes. Muffin tins or pans are available in sets of six or 12 indentations and have deep-set muffin holes. Fairy cake, bun or patty tins have shallower indentations for making smaller cakes. Use finely pleated cake papers to ensure easy release from the tins and to help to keep the cakes fresher. They also make an attractive decorative feature as they are available in a wide variety of pretty colours and patterns – flowery, stripy, dotty, with little red

Above: Use paper cakes to line muffin tins. Paper and foil cases are made in a range of sizes, colours and patterns.

hearts, and more. Make sure that they are non-stick or most of the cake will stick to the paper. Use double cases for neater cakes.

When the cakes are cooked

To check that your cakes are ready, look to see that they are a pale golden colour, risen and firm to the touch when pressed lightly in the centre.

As freshly baked cakes are very fragile, they need time to stand in the tins to cool for a short time to firm them. Small cakes should only be left in the tin for about 3 minutes before releasing onto a wire rack to cool down completely.

Above: Cakes are cooked when they are well risen, a golden colour and feel firm to the touch.

Storing cakes

Make sure that your cakes are completely cold before storing, otherwise condensation will form in the tin and this can cause the cakes to go mouldy, even within a few days. Plastic food containers will help to keep cakes moist although airtight cake tins are necessary for fatless sponge-type cakes. Cakes with fresh cream fillings and decorative toppings need to be kept in the refrigerator and ideally eaten on the day they are filled with cream.

Fillings and toppings

Cakes are made extra special by adding a filling or topping, and there are many different coverings to suit a variety of uses. Use sugarpaste icing on celebration cakes, or frostings on tiny cupcakes, or decorate with simple frosted flowers.

Buttercream icing

This rich icing makes a good covering and filling for little cakes.

MAKES 350G/12OZ/2 CUPS
75g/3oz/6 tbsp butter, softened
225g/8oz/2 cups icing
   (confectioners') sugar, sifted
5ml/1 tsp vanilla extract
10ml/2 tsp milk

Place the butter, icing sugar and vanilla extract in a bowl and whisk or beat with a wooden spoon. Add the milk and beat until soft and fluffy. Store, chilled for up to 2 days.

Ganache

This delicious icing makes a perfect topping or filling for special occasion chocolate cakes.

MAKES 350G/12OZ/2 CUPS
250ml/8fl oz/1 cup double
   (heavy) cream
225g/8oz plain (semisweet)
   chocolate, broken into pieces

Gently heat both ingredients in a pan, stirring constantly until melted. Pour into a clean, dry bowl, leave to cool, then spread over the cakes.

Chocolate fudge frosting

This glossy frosting can be poured over cakes or spread as a filling.

MAKES 350G/12OZ/2 CUPS
115g/4oz plain (semisweet)
   chocolate, broken into pieces
50g/2oz/¼ cup butter, softened
1 egg, beaten
175g/6oz/1½ cups icing
   (confectioners') sugar, sifted
2.5ml/½ tsp vanilla extract

Melt the chocolate and butter in a bowl set over a pan of hot water. Remove from the heat and whisk in the egg, icing sugar and vanilla. Whisk until smooth.

Cook's Tip

You can either use the chocolate fudge frosting at once, or allow it to cool and thicken.

Glacé icing

Also known as water icing, this is the simplest of all icing recipes, and is ideal for decorating small cakes. It's quick to make, with only two basic ingredients, and provided you take care to get the consistency right it flows easily over the surface and sets to a glossy smoothness.

The icing can be flavoured with vanilla, fruit juice and zest, chocolate, coffee or alcohol, and looks wonderful in delicate, pastel colours. It is important to get the consistency exactly right: too thick and it will not form a super-smooth glossy coating; too thin and it will run over the top and down the sides of the cakes. Glacé icing sets to form a crisp surface, but never becomes rock hard.

MAKES 225G/8OZ/2½ CUPS
225g/8oz/2 cups icing
  (confectioners') sugar
a few drops of vanilla extract
30–45ml/2–3 tsp hot water
a few drops of food colouring

Above. The combination of alphabet decorations and tinted glacé icing make these cakes appealing to children.

Sift the icing sugar into a bowl and add the vanilla. Then slowly mix in the water, a few drops at a time, beating until the mixture is the consistency of cream.

Add one or two drops of food colouring (with caution). For a more vibrant colour use paste food colouring, available from specialist suppliers. Stir until the icing is evenly coloured.

Use the icing immediately, while it is smooth and fluid. Add any further decoration to the cakes before the icing dries.

Flavouring variations

Fresh fruit:
The strained juice from fresh berries such as raspberries, redcurrants or citrus fruits can be used to scent and softly colour plain icing and glazes. A more concentrated citrus hit can be achieved by adding finely grated zest or replacing some of the water used to make up the glacé icing with fruit juice.

Alcohol:
Lift the flavour of icing with 15–30ml/2 tbsp crème de framboise (raspberry liqueur), limoncello (lemon liqueur), or another fruit-based liqueur, which will add fruity tones. For a festive treat you could also try adding 15–30ml/2 tbsp brandy or whisky to icing for Christmas cakes.

Coffee:
Dissolve 5ml/1 tsp coffee granules in 15ml/1 tsp of hot water, then cool. Add the coffee to your glacé icing a little at a time to achieve your desired taste.

All kinds of little cakes

This wonderful collection of mini cakes and bakes offers plenty of choice to inspire even the most experienced home baker. With new twists on classics such as baby Madeira cakes and mini Lamingtons, plus irresistible cake pops, chocolate muffins, creamy cupcakes and seasonal whoopie pies, there are plenty of ideas to try for your next birthday party, special afternoon tea or just when you fancy something deliciously sweet and tasty.

Seville orange cakes

A few drops of Grand Marnier will add warmth to the flavour of this sharp-sweet butter frosting. Out of season, a sweet orange may be substituted for the Seville orange. If making these cakes for children omit the Grand Marnier

Makes 9

75g/6oz/¾ cup butter, softened
75g/6oz/¾ cup caster (superfine)
  sugar
4 eggs, lightly beaten
175g/6oz/1¾ cups self-raising
  (self-rising) flour, sifted
candied lemon rind, to decorate

For the Seville orange buttercream

140g/5oz/10 tbsp butter,
  softened
250g/9oz/2¼ cups icing
  (confectioners') sugar
juice and finely grated rind of one
  Seville orange
5ml/1 tsp Grand Marnier
orange food colouring (optional)

1 Preheat the oven to 180°C/350°F/Gas 4. Line 9 cups of a bun tin or pan with paper cases. Place the butter and sugar in a mixing bowl.

2 Beat together using a wooden spoon or an electric mixer until very light and creamy. Gradually add the eggs, beating well after each addition.

3 Add the sifted flour and fold it delicately into the mixture with a large spoon until just combined.

4 Divide the mixture among the paper cases and bake for 20 minutes until the cakes are golden brown and the centres feel firm to the touch. Remove from the oven.

5 Leave to cool for 5 minutes, then turn the cakes out on to a wire rack to cool completely before decorating them.

6 To make the buttercream, beat the softened butter until light and fluffy, using an electric mixer or a wooden spoon.

7 Gradually add the sugar, orange juice and rind, Grand Marnier and a few drops of food colouring, if using, beating continuously until the mixture is smooth.

8 Cover the bowl and chill for several hours to allow the flavours to mature before using as a filling or topping.

9 Using a piping or icing bag with a plain nozzle, pipe the buttercream on to the cakes in the shape of a large dome. Finish off with a few slivers of candied lemon rind.

Energy 554kcal/2319kJ; Protein 5.3g; Carbohydrate 64.7g, of which sugars 50g; Fat 32g, of which saturates 19.1g; Cholesterol 177mg; Calcium 92mg; Fibre 0.8g; Sodium 324mg.

Chocolate chip cakes

Nothing could be easier – or nicer – than these classic muffins. The muffin mixture is plain, but has a delicious layer of chocolate chips inside. Sprinkle a few chocolate chips on top of the cakes to make them look irresistible. They are delicious eaten warm.

Makes 10

115g/4oz/½ cup butter, softened
75g/3oz/⅓ cup caster (superfine) sugar
30ml/2 tbsp soft dark brown sugar
2 eggs
175g/6oz/1½ cups plain (all-purpose) flour
5ml/1 tsp baking powder
120ml/4fl oz/½ cup milk
175g/6oz/1 cup plain (semisweet) chocolate chips

1 Preheat the oven to 190°C/375°F/Gas 5. Arrange 10 paper cases in a muffin tin or pan.

2 In a large bowl, beat the butter until it is pale and light. Add the caster and dark brown sugars and beat until the mixture is light and fluffy. Beat in the eggs, one at a time, beating thoroughly after each addition.

3 Sift the flour and baking powder together twice. Fold into the butter mixture, alternating with the milk.

4 Divide half the mixture among the paper cases. Sprinkle with half the chocolate chips, then cover with the remaining mixture and the rest of the chocolate chips. Bake for about 25 minutes, until golden. Leave to stand for 5 minutes then transfer to a wire rack to cool.

Cook's Tip

For best results, allow the butter and eggs to reach room temperature before beginning the recipe.

Energy 296kcal/1241kJ; Protein 4.2g; Carbohydrate 36.5g, of which sugars 22.3g; Fat 15.9g, of which saturates 9.5g; Cholesterol 67mg; Calcium 59mg; Fibre 0.5g; Sodium 110mg.

Fresh raspberry and fig cakes

Beautiful purple figs, with their luscious red flesh, nestle with fresh raspberries in this delicious cake batter, which puffs up around them in a golden dome as it bakes. Cakes made with fresh summer fruit are a seasonal treat and best eaten while still warm from the oven.

Makes 8–9

140g/5oz/¾ cup fresh raspberries
15ml/1 tbsp caster (superfine) sugar
3 fresh figs
225g/8oz/2 cups plain (all-purpose) flour
10ml/2 tsp baking powder
140g/5oz/¾ cup golden (superfine) caster sugar
85g/3½oz/7 tbsp butter, melted
1 egg, beaten
285ml/½ pint buttermilk
grated rind of ½ small orange

1 Preheat the oven to 180°C/350°F/Gas 4. Grease the cups of a large muffin tin or pan or line with paper muffin cases.

2 Arrange the fresh raspberries in a single layer on a large plate and sprinkle them evenly with the 15ml/1 tbsp caster sugar. Slice the figs vertically into eighths and set them aside with the raspberries.

3 Sift the flour and baking powder into a large mixing bowl and mix in the sugar. Make a well in the centre of the dry ingredients.

4 In another bowl, mix the cooled melted butter with the egg, buttermilk and grated orange rind. Pour this mixture into the dry ingredients and fold in gently until just blended. Do not overwork the mixture.

5 Set aside a small quantity of the raspberries and figs. Sprinkle the remaining fruit over the surface of the batter and fold in lightly. Spoon the mixture into the tin or the paper cases, filling each not more than two-thirds full.

6 Lightly press the reserved fruit into the top of the batter. Bake for 25 minutes until the muffins are risen and golden. Leave in the tin for 5 minutes, then turn out on to a wire rack to cool.

Cook's Tip
These elegant cakes could also be served warm as a dessert, accompanied by crème fraiche.

Energy 260kcal/1098kJ; Protein 4.7g; Carbohydrate 43.2g, of which sugars 24.2g; Fat 8.9g, of which saturates 5.4g; Cholesterol 44mg; Calcium 107mg; Fibre 1.7g; Sodium 102mg.

Citrus syrup cakes

These moist, syrupy cakes, with a very intense tangy citrus flavour, are made without flour, which makes them entirely safe to eat for anyone who has a wheat allergy. To make a luscious dessert add your choice of berries and a scoop of vanilla ice cream.

Makes 12

3 clementines
6 eggs
225g/8oz/1 cup caster
  (superfine) sugar
225g/8oz/2 cups ground almonds
icing (confectioners') sugar, to
  dust

For the citrus syrup

350g/12oz/3 cups caster
  (superfine) sugar
250ml/9fl oz water
rind of 1 clementine, pith
  removed, cut into very fine
  strips
juice of ¾ lemon

1 Put the whole, unpeeled clementines into a pan and cover generously with boiling water. Bring to the boil, then simmer for about 2 hours. This will soften the fruit and remove some of the bitterness from the skin. Keep a check on the water level and top up as necessary with boiling water.

2 Meanwhile, preheat the oven to 160°C/325°F/Gas 3. Set 12 oblong silicone cake cases on a baking sheet, or line a 12-hole bun tin or pan with paper cake cases.

3 Remove the fruit from the water and leave to cool. Split open and discard the pips (seeds). Liquidize the fruit into a purée. Set aside.

4 Whisk the eggs and sugar together until foamy, then stir in the ground almonds and the fruit purée. Pour the mixture into the prepared cases and bake for 30 minutes.

5 To make the syrup, dissolve the sugar in the measured water. Add the strips of rind and the lemon juice and bring to the boil. Reduce the heat and simmer for 2–3 minutes, until the liquid coats the back of a spoon.

6 Allow the cakes to cool in the cases, then drizzle the warm syrup over, a spoonful at a time.

Energy 344kcal/1449kJ; Protein 7.4g; Carbohydrate 52.2g, of which sugars 51.7g; Fat 13.3g, of which saturates 1.7g; Cholesterol 95mg; Calcium 88mg; Fibre 1.5g; Sodium 41mg.

Lemon meringue cakes

This recipe is a delightful amalgam of a traditional fairy cake with the classic lemon meringue pie – soft lemon sponge cake is topped with crisp meringue. The little cakes are lovely with tea, but can also be served hot as a dessert, accompanied by cream or ice cream.

Makes 18

115g/4oz/½ cup butter, softened
200g/7oz/scant 1 cup caster (superfine) sugar
2 eggs
115g/4oz/1 cup self-raising (self-rising) flour
5ml/1 tsp baking powder
grated rind of 2 lemons
30ml/2 tbsp lemon juice
2 egg whites

Cook's Tip

When your egg whites get fluffy stop beating. If you overbeat them, they will liquify again.

1 Preheat the oven to 190°C/375°F/ Gas 5. Arrange 18 paper cases in muffin tins or pans.

2 Put the butter in a bowl and beat until soft. Add 115g/4oz/generous ½ cup of the caster sugar and continue to beat until the mixture is light and creamy. Add the eggs, one at a time, beating thoroughly after each addition until the mixture is smooth.

3 Sift together the flour and baking powder over the creamed mixture, add half the lemon rind and all the lemon juice and beat well until thoroughly combined.

4 Divide the mixture among the paper cases, filling each case about two-thirds full.

5 To make the meringue, whisk the egg whites in a clean, grease-free bowl until they stand in soft peaks. Stir in the remaining caster sugar and lemon rind.

6 Put a spoonful of the meringue mixture on top of each cake. Cook for 20–25 minutes, until the meringue is crisp and brown. Serve the cakes hot or turn out on to a wire rack to cool.

Energy 123kcal/514kJ; Protein 1.7g; Carbohydrate 16.6g, of which sugars 11.7g; Fat 6g, of which saturates 3.5g; Cholesterol 35mg; Calcium 19mg; Fibre 0.2g; Sodium 54mg.

Baby Madeira cakes

This recipe looks as good as it tastes. The Madeira cake mixture, enriched with ground almonds and Calvados, rises beautifully into a perfect dome. When the cakes have cooled the domes are carefully sliced away to make room for a buttercream and raspberry jam filling.

Makes 14

225g/8oz/1 cup butter, softened
225g/8oz/1 cup caster
  (superfine) sugar
4 eggs
225g/8oz/2 cups self-raising
  (self-rising) flour
115g/4oz/1 cup plain (all-
  purpose) flour
60ml/4 tbsp ground almonds
5ml/1 tsp finely grated lemon
  rind
30ml/2 tbsp Calvados, brandy
  or milk

For the filling
175g/6oz/¾ cup butter, softened
350g/12oz/3 cups icing
  (confectioners') sugar, sifted,
  plus extra for dusting
20ml/4 tsp lemon juice
20ml/4 tsp warm water
60ml/4 tbsp raspberry jam

1 Preheat the oven to 180°C/350°F/ Gas 4. Line 14 cups of two muffin tins or pans with paper cases.

2 Cream the butter and caster sugar together until light and fluffy.

3 Add two of the eggs, a little at a time, mixing well after each addition. Sprinkle 15ml/1 tbsp of the flour into the mixture and beat it in. Add the remaining eggs gradually, beating well after each addition, then beat in another 15ml/1 tbsp flour until just combined. Sift the remaining flours into the mixture and fold in lightly with the ground almonds, lemon rind and Calvados, brandy or milk.

4 Fill the prepared cups almost to the top. Bake for 20–22 minutes until the tops spring back when touched and the cakes are light golden. Transfer to a wire rack.

5 To make the buttercream, beat the softened butter with the icing sugar until it is smooth and fluffy. Stir in the lemon juice and warm water and continue to beat until smooth.

6 When the cakes have cooled completely, slice a round from the top of each cake.

7 Using a large piping or pastry bag fitted with a plain nozzle, pipe a circle of buttercream.

8 Add a spoonful of jam to fill each cake before replacing the dome on top. Just before serving, dust lightly with sifted icing sugar.

Energy 574kcal/2406kJ; Protein 5.2g; Carbohydrate 75.5g, of which sugars 54g; Fat 29.5g, of which saturates 18.6g; Cholesterol 140mg; Calcium 81mg; Fibre 0.9g; Sodium 278mg.

Fondant fancies

A classic fondant coating is light and shiny, and ideal to finish these delicate little cakes. These fancies are very pretty, so serve them for a celebration such as a christening. They will keep for two days in an airtight container.

Makes 28

50g/2oz/½ cup butter, melted
oil, for greasing
3 large (US extra large) eggs
100g/3¾oz/generous ½ cup
   caster (superfine) sugar
100g/3¾oz/scant 1 cup plain
   (all-purpose) flour
15ml/1 tbsp cornflour
   (cornstarch)
pinch of salt

For the icing and decoration
500g/1lb/5 cups fondant icing
   sugar, sifted
food colourings

Cook's Tip
The undecorated base could be frozen for up to three months. Allow to cool completely then wrap in strong freezer film or foil and label. Unwrap and allow to thaw at room temperature before using.

1 Preheat the oven to 180°C/350°F/Gas 4. Oil and line a 28 × 18cm/11 × 7in baking tin with baking parchment.

2 Whisk the eggs and sugar together, using an electric mixer, until pale and creamy, and the mixture leaves a trail when the beaters are lifted away.

3 Sift the flour, cornflour and salt over the surface and pour the melted butter around the sides of the bowl. Gently fold together, taking care not to knock out the air, then pour into the lined tin.

4 Bake for 20 minutes, or until light golden and just firm to the touch.

5 Cool in the tin for 5 minutes, then turn out, peel away the lining paper and leave on a wire rack until cold.

6 Stamp out small squares, and put on a wire rack standing over a tray.

7 Put the sifted fondant icing sugar into a bowl and mix in enough cold water to give a coating consistency. Divide the icing among several bowls and colour it delicately with a few drops of food colouring. Keep each bowl covered with a damp cloth until needed.

8 Working quickly, spoon the icing over each cake and smooth down to cover the tops and sides. When dry, put in paper cases to serve.

Energy 259kcal/1094kJ; Protein 2.7g; Carbohydrate 49.7g, of which sugars 41.4g; Fat 6.9g, of which saturates 4g; Cholesterol 40mg; Calcium 50mg; Fibre 0.3g; Sodium 66mg.

Chocolate fairy cakes

These magical little treats are sure to enchant adults and children alike. The chocolate sponge is rich, moist and dark, and contrasts appetizingly with the pure white vanilla-flavoured buttercream, which is swirled generously over the top.

Makes 24

175g/6oz/¾ cup butter, softened
150ml/¼ pint/⅔ cup milk
5ml/1 tsp vanilla extract
115g/4oz plain (semisweet)
  chocolate, broken into pieces
15ml/1 tbsp water
275g/10oz/2½ cups plain (all-
  purpose) flour
5ml/1 tsp baking powder
2.5ml/½ tsp bicarbonate of soda
  (baking soda)
300g/11oz/1½ cups caster
  (superfine) sugar
3 eggs

For the vanilla icing
40g/1½oz/3 tbsp butter
115g/4oz/1 cup icing
  (confectioners') sugar
2.5ml/½ tsp vanilla extract
15–30ml/1–2 tbsp milk

1 Preheat the oven to 180°C/350°F/ Gas 4. Arrange 24 paper cases in muffin tins or pans, or grease the cups of the tins.

2 In a large mixing bowl, beat the butter with an electric mixer until it is light and fluffy. Beat in the milk and the vanilla extract.

3 Melt the chocolate with the water in a heatproof bowl set over a pan of simmering water, then add to the butter mixture.

4 Sift the flour, baking powder, bicarbonate of soda and sugar over the batter in batches and stir in. Add the eggs, one at a time; beat well after each addition.

5 Divide the mixture evenly among the muffin cases. Bake for 20–25 minutes or until a skewer inserted into the centre comes out clean. Turn out to cool on a wire rack.

6 To make the icing, beat the butter with the icing sugar and vanilla extract. Add just enough milk to make a creamy mixture. Spread on top of the cooled cakes.

Energy 210kcal/884kJ; Protein 2.5g; Carbohydrate 30.4g, of which sugars 21.6g; Fat 9.7g, of which saturates 5.8g; Cholesterol 44mg; Calcium 39mg; Fibre 0.5g; Sodium 67mg.

Mini party cakes

These little cakes look extremely pretty decorated with icing and sugarpaste ornaments in different pastel colours. Once the cakes are iced a sherbet 'flying saucer' sweet is stuck on top of each one, before being decorated with butterflies and flowers.

Makes 48

175g/6oz/¾ cup butter, softened
175g/6oz/¾ cup caster
  (superfine) sugar
4 eggs, lightly beaten
5ml/1 tsp vanilla extract
175g/6oz/1½ cups self-raising
  (self-rising) flour, sifted
sherbet-filled flying saucer sweets
  and sugarpaste decorations, to
  decorate

For the icing
150g/5oz/1¼ cups icing
  (confectioners') sugar, sifted
food colouring in 4 colours: pink,
  pale blue, peach, green

1 Preheat the oven to 180°C/350°F/ Gas 4. Line the cups of four 12-cup mini cupcake trays with paper cases.

2 Place the softened butter and sugar in the bowl of an electric mixer and beat until light and creamy. Gradually add the eggs in small amounts, beating well after each addition.

3 Add the vanilla and sifted flour and fold it into the butter mixture until just combined.

4 Half-fill the paper cases with the mixture and bake for 12–15 minutes until golden. Test by pressing the centre of the cakes with your finger: the sponge should lightly spring back. Leave on a wire rack to cool completely.

5 Make the icing with just enough hot water (about 20ml/4 tsp) to make a soft glacé icing. Divide the icing between four bowls, then tint each with a different food colour, keeping the colours pale.

6 Ice each cake and coax it to the edges with the back of the spoon.

7 Decorate flying saucer sweets with tinted sprinkles and sugarpaste flowers, leaves and butterflies. Attach with glacé icing. Stick each saucer to the top of a cupcake with glacé icing.

Energy 78kcal/329kJ; Protein 0.9g; Carbohydrate 11.6g, of which sugars 8.9g; Fat 3.5g, of which saturates 2.1g; Cholesterol 24mg; Calcium 20mg; Fibre 0.1g; Sodium 47mg.

Blackberry and almond muffins

Sloe gin and rose water add depth of flavour to these muffins, helping them to stand out from the crowd. Autumnal blackberries are perfectly complemented by the mild flavour and crunch of blanched almonds. Store in an airtight container for up to three days.

Makes 12 standard muffins

100g/3½oz/scant 1 cup fresh blackberries
300g/11oz/2¾ cups plain (all-purpose) flour
50g/2oz/¼ cup soft light brown sugar
20ml/4 tsp baking powder
60g/2¼oz/⅓ cup blanched almonds, chopped
2 eggs
100ml/3½fl oz/scant ½ cup milk
50g/2oz/¼ cup butter, melted
15ml/1 tbsp sloe gin
15ml/1 tbsp rose water

1 Preheat the oven to 200°C/400°F/Gas 6. Line the cups of a muffin tin or pan with paper cases.
2 Rinse the blackberries in a colander and pat dry.
3 Sift the flour, sugar and baking powder into a large bowl.
4 Stir in the almonds and blackberries, mixing them well to coat with the flour mixture. Make a well in the centre of the dry ingredients.
5 In another bowl, whisk the eggs with the milk, then mix in the butter, sloe gin and rose water. Add to the dry ingredients and stir in.
6 Spoon the batter into the prepared paper cases and bake for 20–25 minutes or until golden.
7 Leave to stand for 5 minutes before turning out on to a wire rack to cool. Serve with butter, if you like.

Cook's Tip
One of the joys of autumn is gathering blackberries from the hedgerows. Rinsing them in a large bowl of water with 15ml/1 tbsp vinegar will ensure any little bugs are removed.

Energy 181kcal/761kJ; Protein 4.8g; Carbohydrate 25g, of which sugars 5.8g; Fat 7.6g, of which saturates 2.9g; Cholesterol 42mg; Calcium 68mg; Fibre 1.4g; Sodium 49mg.

Apple and Calvados muffins with quince

A simple apple muffin is transformed into something grander with the addition of luxurious French apple brandy and the aromatic flavour of quince. Quince glaze gives an appetizing shine to these wonderful muffins. Store in an airtight container for up to three days.

Makes 10

250g/9oz/1¼ cups peeled and cored cooking apple
30–45ml/2–3 tbsp quince paste
75g/3oz/6 tbsp butter
15ml/1 tbsp Calvados
225g/8oz/2 cups plain (all-purpose) flour
12.5ml/2½ tsp baking powder
85g/3oz/scant ⅓ cup caster (superfine) sugar
1 egg, lightly beaten
60ml/4 tbsp buttermilk
grated rind of 1 lemon

For the quince glaze
45ml/3 tbsp quince paste
5ml/1 tsp lemon juice
30ml/2 tbsp Calvados

1 Preheat the oven to 180°C /350°F/Gas 4. Line the cups of a muffin tin or pan with paper cases.

2 Chop most of the apples into cubes, and set aside. Cut a few into crescents and put in lemon water.

3 Put the quince paste and butter in a pan and stir until melted. Remove from the heat. Add the Calvados.

4 Sift the flour, baking powder and sugar into a large bowl and form a well in the centre. Blend the egg and buttermilk. Pour into the dry ingredients with the lemon rind, Calvados mixture and apple. Stir until just blended.

5 Spoon the batter into the paper cases. Drain and slice the reserved apple segments into thin pieces and lightly press several on each muffin.

6 Bake for 25–30 minutes until golden and springy to the touch. Leave to stand for a few minutes then transfer to a wire rack.

7 To make the quince glaze, add the quince paste, lemon juice and 15ml/ 1 tbsp water to a small pan. Boil rapidly to make a thin syrup. Stir in the Calvados and simmer for 1 minute. Brush thickly over the surface of the warm muffins.

Energy 213kcal/899kJ; Protein 3.1g; Carbohydrate 34.1g, of which sugars 16.9g; Fat 7.1g, of which saturates 4.3g; Cholesterol 37mg; Calcium 50mg; Fibre 1.1g; Sodium 70mg.

Queen of Hearts mini sandwich cakes

These heart-shaped Victoria sponges will be a hit at any tea-time party. It is possible to get textured rolling pins to produce a textured finish to the ready-to-roll fondant icing, but also look around the house for items that can be used to produce a pretty texture.

Makes 8 mini sandwich cakes

For the cakes
115g/4oz/½ cup butter
115g/4oz/generous ½ cup caster (superfine) sugar
2 eggs, lightly beaten
115g/4oz/1 cup self-raising (self-rising) flour, sifted
grated rind of 1 lemon
15–30ml/1–2 tbsp lemon juice

For the decoration
50g/2oz ready-to-roll fondant icing, red
a piece of light card
90g/3½oz/⅓ cup raspberry jam
150g/5oz/1¼ cups icing (confectioners') sugar, sifted
15–30ml/1–2 tbsp lemon juice
edible glitter (optional)

1 Preheat the oven to 180°C/350°F/Gas 4. Lightly grease a 8-cup heart-shaped silicone mould and dust with a little flour. Stand the mould on a baking sheet.

2 Cream the butter for a few minutes until soft and pale. Add the sugar and continue to beat until the mixture is pale and fluffy. Gradually add the lightly beaten eggs to the butter and sugar mixture, beating well between each addition. Add a teaspoonful of flour with each of the last two additions, so that the mixture does not curdle. Fold in the sifted flour and the grated rind, then add the juice, a little at a time, until the mixture drops slowly off the spoon.

3 Divide the mixture between the moulds, filling to about half to two-thirds full. Bake for 20–25 minutes. Allow to cool in the moulds for a couple of minutes, then transfer to a wire rack.

4 Roll out the red ready-to-roll fondant icing and then use a pastry or cookie cutter to mark lines to look like quilting. Cut out 8 hearts with a cutter about 2.5cm/1in deep. Fold the piece of card into a gutter shape, grease lightly and rest the hearts so that they curve upwards. Set the hearts aside to dry.

5 When the cakes are quite cold, cut them in half with a sharp knife and sandwich together with jam. Mix the icing sugar with lemon juice, 5ml/1 tsp at a time until it is just thin enough to spread over the cakes. Brush loose crumbs off the cakes, then spread the icing over, allowing it to drizzle down the sides, and then position a heart on the top. Dust each cake with a pinch of edible glitter, if you like.

Energy 358kcal/1507kJ; Protein 3g; Carbohydrate 59g, of which sugars 48g; Fat 14g, of which saturates 8g; Cholesterol 90mg; Calcium 65mg; Fibre 1g; Sodium 168mg

Flutterby butterfly cakes

The method of scooping a disc out of the top of the cupcake and cutting it in two to form butterfly wings can be used with any sort of cupcake; some people use jam to hold the wings together but to ring the changes lemon buttercream is used in this recipe.

Makes 12

For the cakes
115g/4oz/½ cup butter
115g/4oz/generous ½ cup caster (superfine) sugar
2 eggs, lightly beaten
115g/4oz/1 cup self-raising (self-rising) flour, sifted
finely grated rind of 1 lemon
15–30ml/1–2 tbsp lemon juice

For the decoration
a sheet of light card
75g/3oz ready-to-roll fondant icing, white
gel or paste food colouring, pink and blue
edible pearls
50g/2oz/¼ cup butter
115g/4oz/1 cup icing (confectioners') sugar, sifted
5ml/1 tsp lemon juice

1 Preheat the oven to 180°C/350°F/Gas 4. Line a muffin tin or pan with cupcake cases.

2 Cream the butter for a few minutes until soft and pale. Add the sugar, and continue to beat until the mixture is pale and fluffy. Gradually add the eggs, beating well between each addition. Add a teaspoonful of flour with the last two additions so that the mixture does not curdle. Fold in the sifted flour and the lemon rind, then add the lemon juice, a little at a time, until the mixture drops slowly off the spoon.

3 Divide the mixture between the cupcake cases. Bake for 20–25 minutes until risen, lightly browned and bouncy to the touch. Allow to cool in the tin for a couple of minutes, then transfer to a wire rack to cool completely.

4 For the decoration, fold the sheet of card lengthways into four to form a gutter and grease lightly. Colour half the ready-to-roll fondant icing pale pink and the other half pale blue. Roll out and cut butterfly shapes about 4.5cm/1¾in across. Crease lightly along the centre and place in the folded paper gutter. Press edible pearls into each wing and leave to dry.

5 Cream the butter for a few minutes until soft and pale. Gradually add the sifted icing sugar, beating well between each addition. Beat in 5ml/1tsp of lemon juice.

6 Cut a shallow, circular scoop out of the top of each cake. Put a teaspoonful of buttercream into each scoop. Cut the pieces of cake in two and place on the top of the buttercream to form wings. Position an icing butterfly on top of each cake.

Energy 246kcal/1030kJ; Protein 2g; Carbohydrate 33g, of which sugars 26g; Fat 13g, of which saturates 7g; Cholesterol 69mg; Calcium 44mg; Fibre 0g; Sodium 136mg

Mini Victoria sponge pops

The Victoria sponge is one of England's most popular teatime treats – light vanilla cakes sandwiched together with buttercream and jam, and elegantly dusted with icing sugar. These mini versions are perfect for serving with a pot of freshly brewed tea.

Makes 10

For the cakes
50g/2oz/¼ cup butter, softened
50g/2oz/¼ cup caster (superfine) sugar
1 egg
5ml/1 tsp vanilla extract
50g/2oz/½ cup self-raising (self-rising) flour, sifted
5ml/1 tsp baking powder

For the buttercream and jam filling
100g/3¾oz/scant 1 cup icing (confectioners') sugar, plus extra for dusting
30g/1¼oz/2½ tbsp butter, softened
30g/1¼oz/scant ¼ cup cream cheese
5ml/1 tsp vanilla extract
a little milk, for mixing (optional)
60–75ml/4–5 tbsp good quality strawberry jam
10 lollipop sticks, to serve
10 tiny ribbons (optional)

1 Preheat the oven to 180°C/350°F/Gas 4. Grease a 10-cup straight-sided mini muffin tin, pan or silicone mould. To make the cakes, cream the butter and sugar together until fluffy. Beat in the egg and vanilla extract.

2 Sift the flour and baking powder into the butter mixture, then fold in. Divide the cake mixture between the cups of the prepared tin or mould. Bake for 12–15 minutes, until the cakes spring back when gently pressed. Transfer to a wire rack to cool

3 For the buttercream, sift the icing sugar into a bowl, add the butter, cream cheese and vanilla extract, and whisk together for 3 minutes, or until light and creamy, adding a little milk if necessary.

4 Cut each of the cakes in half horizontally. Using a piping or pastry bag fitted with a small star-shaped nozzle, pipe the buttercream on to the bottom half of each cake. Using a teaspoon, add a little strawberry jam to each. Top with the other cake halves and dust with sifted icing sugar. Insert a wooden skewer into the top of each cake and tie a ribbon around it.

Energy 177kcal/742kJ; Protein 2g; Carbohydrate 24g, of which sugars 20g; Fat 9g, of which saturates 5g; Cholesterol 45mg; Calcium 33mg; Fibre 0.3g; Sodium 136mg.

Chocolate truffle muffins

Not an everyday muffin, these luscious chocolate treats with a hidden truffle centre and equally sinful soft chocolate frosting are decorated with pretty seashell chocolates. The chocolates can be bought or you could make your own using plastic moulds. Eat fresh.

Makes 9

165g/5½oz/scant ¾ cup
  butter, softened
150g/5oz/⅔ cup light muscovado
  (brown) sugar
3 eggs, lightly beaten
150g/5oz self-raising
  (self-rising) flour
25g/1oz/¼ cup unsweetened
  cocoa powder
7.5ml/1½ tsp baking powder
chocolate seashells, to decorate

For the truffles

150g/5oz dark (bittersweet)
  chocolate, broken into pieces
20ml/4 tsp double (heavy) cream
20ml/4 tsp brandy (optional)

For the frosting

250ml/8fl oz/1 cup double
  (heavy) cream
75g/3oz/⅓ cup soft brown sugar
5ml/1 tsp vanilla extract
150g/5oz dark (bittersweet)
  chocolate, grated

1 Preheat the oven to 180°C/350°F/Gas 4. Line the cups of a muffin tin or pan with paper cases.

2 To make the truffles, melt the chocolate in a heatproof bowl set over a pan of simmering water. Remove from the heat, and stir in the cream and the alcohol. Set aside to cool and thicken.

3 Scoop the cool mixture into 9 balls.

4 To make the muffins, beat the butter and sugar in a bowl. Beat in the eggs. Sift in the flour, cocoa and baking powder and mix lightly.

5 Half fill the paper cases. Add a truffle to the centre. Spoon the remaining cake batter on top.

6 Bake for 22–25 minutes or until risen and springy to the touch. Cool.

7 For the frosting, put the cream, sugar and vanilla in a pan and heat until it reaches boiling point. Remove from the heat. Stir in the chocolate until melted. Cool.

8 Spread on top of cold muffins and decorate with chocolate seashells.

Energy 331kcal/1381kJ; Protein 3.6g; Carbohydrate 28.6g, of which sugars 27.4g; Fat 23.5g, of which saturates 14.3g; Cholesterol 110mg; Calcium 32mg; Fibre 0.3g; Sodium 191mg.

Marshmallow daisy cakes

These lemony cakes are as fresh as a daisy; they are quick and very simple to make and bake. The marshmallow flowers take moments to create – all you need is a pair of scissors. They are sure to be a hit, especially with children, and will keep for two days in an airtight container.

Makes 12

115g/4oz/1 cup self-raising (self-rising) flour
5ml/1 tsp baking powder
115g/4oz/generous ½ cup caster (superfine) sugar
115g/4oz/½ cup soft tub margarine
2 large (US extra large) eggs, beaten
15ml/1 tbsp lemon juice
finely grated rind of 1 lemon

For the decoration
½ quantity buttercream, see page 10
12 pink and white marshmallows
caster (superfine) sugar, for dusting
small sweets or candies

1 Preheat the oven to 180°C/350°F/Gas 4. Line a 12-cup muffin tin or pan with paper cases.
2 Sift the flour, baking powder and sugar into a large bowl, then add the remaining ingredients. Beat until light and creamy, then place heaped spoonfuls into the paper cases.
3 Bake for about 20 minutes, or until golden and firm to the touch. Allow to cool for 2 minutes, then turn out on to a wire rack to go cold.
4 When cold, spread the top of each cake with a little buttercream.
5 Use kitchen scissors to cut each marshmallow in half horizontally. Dip the cut marshmallow edges in caster sugar to prevent sticking. Repeat, cutting the marshmallows in half again, and dipping the cut edge in caster sugar.
6 Press the tips of four halves together to form four petals of a flower. Arrange them on top of a cupcake and press a small sweet into the centre.

Energy 115kcal/483kJ; Protein 1.3g; Carbohydrate 16.5g, of which sugars 12.1g; Fat 5.4g, of which saturates 3.2g; Cholesterol 31mg; Calcium 18mg; Fibre 0.2g; Sodium 43mg.

Mini Lamingtons

For these tasty squares it is best to use cake that is a day old. Bake the base the day before, then it will cut more easily into squares. Keep a slab in the deep freeze, ready for thawing, cutting and coating. Eat them fresh once decorated.

Makes 24 squares

150g/5oz/generous ½ cup butter, softened, plus extra for greasing
200g/7oz/1 cup caster (superfine) sugar
3 eggs, beaten
300g/11oz/2¾ cups self-raising (self-rising) flour, plus extra for dusting
5ml/1 tsp vanilla extract
150ml/¼ pint/⅔ cup milk

For the icing and decoration
675g/1½lb/3½ cups caster (superfine) sugar
30ml/2 tbsp unsweetened cocoa powder
150g/5oz/1⅔ cups desiccated (dry unsweetened shredded) coconut

1 Preheat the oven to 180°C/350°F/Gas 4. Grease a 20 × 30cm/8 × 12in deep cake tin or pan and dust it lightly with a little flour.

2 Beat the butter and sugar together. Beat in the eggs in batches, adding 5ml/1 tsp flour with each addition to prevent the mixture from curdling.

3 Sift in the remaining flour, then fold into the mixture. Add the vanilla and milk, and mix to a soft, dropping consistency. Spoon into the tin and smooth level, then bake for 30 minutes, or until golden and firm to touch.

4 Cool in the tin for 5 minutes, then turn out on to a wire rack to go cold. Store, wrapped in foil, for 1 day.

5 To make the icing, put the sugar, cocoa and 250ml/8fl oz/1 cup water in a large pan. Heat over a low heat until the sugar has dissolved. Bring to the boil, then simmer, without stirring, for about 12 minutes, or until thickened into a syrup.

6 Put the coconut into a large bowl.

7 Cut the cake into 5cm/2in cubes. Stab a cake cube with a fork and dip into the chocolate icing to coat all over. Coat the cube in the coconut and put on a tray to dry. Repeat with the remaining cakes.

Energy 273kcal/1140kJ; Protein 3.1g; Carbohydrate 28.7g, of which sugars 22.4g; Fat 17g, of which saturates 12.2g; Cholesterol 44mg; Calcium 59mg; Fibre 2.3g; Sodium 160mg.

Sugar sparkle cakes

These delicate rose-flavoured cakes are pretty in pink and perfect for a girls-only party. Make the cakes ahead, if you like, and have fun decorating them with sugar sprinkles, sugar flowers or shapes in your choice of colours. Keep for up to two days in an airtight container.

Makes 12

115g/4oz/1 cup self-raising (self-rising) flour
115g/4oz/generous ½ cup caster (superfine) sugar
115g/4oz/½ cup unsalted butter, softened
2 eggs
15ml/1 tbsp rose water
15ml/1 tbsp milk
pink food colouring, optional

For the topping and decoration
225g/8oz/2 cups icing (confectioners') sugar, sifted
15ml/1 tbsp rose water
pink sugar sprinkles, or sugar flowers or shapes

1 Preheat the oven to 190°C/375°F/Gas 5. Line a 12-cup muffin tin or pan with paper cases.

2 Put the flour, sugar, butter and eggs into a large bowl with the rose water and beat until smooth. Add the milk and a few drops of pink food colouring. Divide among the paper cases.

3 Bake for 15–20 minutes, or until the cakes are risen and golden, and are just firm to the touch. Remove them from the tray and put on a wire rack to cool.

4 To make the topping, sift the icing sugar into a bowl. Add the rose water with a few drops of pink food colouring and 5ml/1 tsp cold water, or enough to mix to a spreadable icing.

5 Spoon a little icing over the top of each cake, then top with sugar sprinkles, flowers or shapes.

Energy 249kcal/1041kJ; Protein 2.4g; Carbohydrate 27g, of which sugars 20.4g; Fat 16.5g, of which saturates 9.5g; Cholesterol 76mg; Calcium 35mg; Fibre 0.3g; Sodium 89mg.

Raspberry and almond cakes

These distinctive, easy-to-make cakes originate from Finland where they are called Runeberg cakes after the famous poet Johan Ludvig Runeberg. The addition of ground almonds, almond liqueur and raspberry jam make them a sophisticated tea-time treat.

Makes 12

175g/6oz/1½ cups plain (all-purpose) flour
5ml/1 tsp baking powder
2 eggs
150g/5oz/¾ cup caster (superfine) sugar
200g/7oz/scant 1 cup unsalted butter, plus extra for greasing
90g/3½oz/scant 1 cup ground almonds
125g/4¼oz/generous 2 cups fine fresh breadcrumbs
about 75ml/5 tbsp almond liqueur, such as Amaretto di Sarone (optional)
150g/5oz/½ cup raspberry jam

1 Preheat the oven to 200°C/400°F/Gas 6. Grease 12 dariol or castle pudding tins or pans.

2 Sift the flour and baking powder together into a bowl. Put the eggs and sugar in a large bowl and whisk together until light and fluffy.

3 In a separate bowl, beat the butter until creamy, then beat in the ground almonds and breadcrumbs. Add the mixture to the eggs and sugar and mix together, then stir in the sifted flour.

4 Divide the mixture between the prepared tins, allowing some room for the mixture to rise. Bake in the oven for 15–20 minutes, until a skewer inserted in the middle comes out clean. Leave to cool in the tins before turning out.

5 Brush the cakes with liqueur to dampen them, and then top each with a teaspoonful of raspberry jam.

Energy 370kcal/1551kJ; Protein 5.4g; Carbohydrate 43.2g, of which sugars 24.1g; Fat 19.2g, of which saturates 9.3g; Cholesterol 67mg; Calcium 68mg; Fibre 1.2g; Sodium 198mg.

Blackcurrant muffins with scarlet frosting

Part-cooking the blackcurrants in sugar and redcurrant jelly adds a pleasant tart-sweet flavour to the fruit. The warm syrupy juices left over from the cooked fruit are combined with icing sugar to make a luscious crimson frosting to spread over the tops of the muffins.

Makes 9–10

75g/3oz/scant ½ cup caster (superfine) sugar
30ml/2 tbsp redcurrant jelly
25g/1oz/2 tbsp butter
225g/8oz/2 cups blackcurrants, topped and tailed, plus extra to decorate
225g/8oz/2 cups plain (all-purpose) flour
12.5ml/2½ tsp baking powder
150g/5oz/scant ¾ cup golden caster (superfine) sugar
75g/3oz/6 tbsp butter, melted
1 egg, lightly beaten
200ml/7fl oz/scant 1 cup buttermilk and milk mixed in equal quantities
5ml/1 tsp grated orange rind
icing (confectioners') sugar

1 Preheat the oven to 190°C/375°F/Gas 5. Line the cups of a muffin tin or pan with paper cases.

2 To prepare the fruit, dissolve the sugar, jelly and butter into a syrup, in a small pan, over a low heat.

3 Set aside the blackcurrants for decoration. Put the rest in a baking tin or pan and pour the syrup over.

4 Bake for 8 minutes, stirring once. Set aside to cool. Turn the oven temperature down to 180°C/350°F/Gas 4.

5 Sift the flour and baking powder into a large bowl and add the sugar. Make a well in the centre. Add the butter, egg, buttermilk mixture and orange rind. Fold in until partly blended.

6 Blend the cooled fruit into the batter, reserving the syrup. Three-quarters fill the paper cases and bake for 22–25 minutes. Turn out on to a wire rack and leave to cool.

7 Mix the reserved syrup with enough icing sugar to make a soft frosting. Swirl the frosting over the cooled muffins. Add a few extra berries and serve immediately.

Energy 208kcal/875kJ; Protein 3.7g; Carbohydrate 29.9g, of which sugars 12.7g; Fat 9.1g, of which saturates 5.6g; Cholesterol 43mg; Calcium 78mg; Fibre 1.5g; Sodium 95mg.

Snowballs

These snowy muffins have the tastiest topping ever: white chocolate mixed with coconut liqueur and cream, then sprinkled with coconut strands. They make an irresistible winter's treat. Keep for up to two days in an airtight container.

Makes 12

175g/6oz/12 tbsp caster (superfine) sugar
2.5ml/½ tsp baking powder
200g/7oz/1¾ cups self-raising (self-rising) flour
15ml/2 tbsp desiccated (dry unsweetened shredded) coconut
175g/6oz/¾ cup soft tub margarine
3 eggs, beaten
15ml/1 tbsp milk

For the topping
175g/6oz white chocolate, chopped
15ml/1 tbsp coconut liqueur
75ml/5 tbsp double (heavy) cream
175g/6oz/2 cups large shredded coconut strands or curls

1 Preheat the oven to 180°C/350°F/Gas 4. Line a 12-cup deep muffin tin or pan with paper cases.
2 Sift the sugar, baking powder, flour and coconut into a large bowl. Add the margarine, eggs and milk and beat until smooth and creamy. Divide the batter evenly among the paper cases.
3 Bake for 18–20 minutes, or until risen, golden and firm to the touch. Leave in the tin for 2 minutes, then turn out to cool on a wire rack.
4 To make the topping, put the chocolate and liqueur in a bowl. Put the cream in a pan and bring to the boil, then pour it over the chocolate and liqueur. Stir until smooth, then cool and chill for 30 minutes.
5 Whisk with an electric mixer for a few minutes, or until light and fluffy.
6 Spread the icing over the top of each muffin, then sprinkle coconut strands liberally over the icing to cover completely.

Energy 481kcal/2005kJ; Protein 5.9g; Carbohydrate 39.6g, of which sugars 35.2g; Fat 34.3g, of which saturates 23.9g; Cholesterol 12mg; Calcium 137mg; Fibre 3g; Sodium 167mg.

Red velvet pops

Red velvet cake is an all-time American classic. Dainty cupcakes are coloured red and flavoured with cocoa to give them their distinctive look. Each cupcake is topped with a swirl of cream cheese icing which has a lovely sharpness to complement the sweet sponge cake.

Makes 20

50g/2oz/¼ cup butter, softened
50g/2oz/¼ cup caster (superfine) sugar
1 egg
45g/1¾oz/scant ½ cup self-raising (self-rising) flour, sifted
15g/½oz unsweetened cocoa powder, sifted, plus extra for dusting
15ml/1 tbsp buttermilk
a few drops of red food colouring gel

For the cream cheese icing

200g/7oz/1¾ cups icing (confectioners') sugar
50g/2oz white chocolate, melted and cooled
30g/1¼oz/scant ¼ cup cream cheese
15ml/1 tbsp buttermilk
20 wooden skewers, to serve
20 mini marshmallows (optional)

1 Preheat the oven to 180°C/350°F/Gas 4. Grease a 24-cup mini muffin tin or pan. To make the cakes, cream the butter and caster sugar together until light and fluffy, then beat in the egg.

2 Sift the flour and cocoa powder together in a separate bowl, then fold into the butter mixture with the buttermilk and a few drops of red food colouring gel (enough to colour the mixture an even reddish brown).

3 Divide the cake mixture between 20 cups of the prepared mini muffin tin. Bake for 12–15 minutes, or until the cakes spring back when gently pressed. Transfer to a wire rack to cool.

4 For the icing, sift the icing sugar into a bowl, add the white chocolate, cream cheese and buttermilk, and whisk for 3 minutes, or until creamy.

5 Using a piping or pastry bag fitted with a large star-shaped nozzle, pipe a swirl of icing on top of each cake. Dust with a little sifted cocoa powder and, when ready to serve, insert a wooden skewer into the base of each cake, securing with a mini marshmallow, if necessary.

Energy 103kcal/433 kJ; Protein 1g; Carbohydrate 16g, of which sugars 15g; Fat 4g, of which saturates 2g; Cholesterol 20mg; Calcium 22mg; Fibre 0.1g; Sodium 44mg.

Orange poppy seed muffins

These muffins look attractive baked in muffin cups and without paper cases so that the poppy-seed flecked sides of the cakes are visible. To serve, break open the muffin and spread with butter and marmalade. Store without icing in an airtight container for three days.

Makes 8

275g/10oz/2½ cups plain
(all-purpose) flour
150g/5oz/¾ cup caster
(superfine) sugar
15ml/1 tbsp baking powder
2 eggs
75g/3oz/6 tbsp butter, melted
75ml/5 tbsp vegetable oil
20–25ml/1½ tbsp poppy seeds
30ml/2tbsp orange juice, plus
grated rind of 1½ oranges
5ml/1 tsp lemon juice, plus
grated rind of 1 lemon

For the icing
25g/1oz/¼ cup icing
(confectioners') sugar
15ml/1 tbsp orange juice

1 Lightly grease the cups of a muffin tin or pan with melted butter or line them with paper cases.
2 Set aside 40g/1½oz of flour. Place the remaining flour with the sugar and baking powder in a mixing bowl. Make a well in the centre.
3 Mix the eggs, butter, oil, poppy seeds, citrus juices and rinds. Pour over the dry ingredients. Fold in until just mixed. Leave for 1 hour.
4 Preheat the oven to 180°C/350°F/Gas 4. Fold the reserved flour into the batter but leave it lumpy.
5 Fill the muffin cups three-quarters full. Bake for 25 minutes, until risen and golden.
6 Leave to stand in the tin for a few minutes, then turn out on to a wire rack to go cold.
7 To make the icing, mix the icing sugar and orange juice in a bowl. Add a small quantity of water, if needed, to make a runny consistency. Drizzle over the cakes.

Energy 377kcal/1583kJ; Protein 5.7g; Carbohydrate 50.7g, of which sugars 24.5g; Fat 18.3g, of which saturates 7.5g; Cholesterol 89mg; Calcium 85mg; Fibre 1.2g; Sodium 107mg.

Christmas cake whoopie pies

These whoopie pies are flavoursome and festive, bursting with fruit and spices. Filled with marshmallow, drizzled with brandy and topped with royal icing and red and silver balls, they embody all the joy of a Christmas cake within a few bites of whoopie pie.

Makes 12

125g/4¼oz/8½ tbsp butter
175g/6oz/¾ cup soft light brown sugar
1 egg
300g/11oz/2¾ cups plain (all-purpose) flour
7.5ml/1½ tsp bicarbonate of soda (baking soda)
5ml/1 tsp salt
2.5ml/½ tsp ground mixed (apple pie) spice
2.5ml/½ tsp ground cinnamon
finely grated rind of 1 orange
250ml/8fl oz/1 cup buttermilk
100g/3¾oz/⅔ cup mixed dried fruit
175g/6oz ready-made marshmallow creme or 'fluff'

For the topping
100ml/3½fl oz/½ cup brandy
150g/5oz/1¼ cups royal icing (confectioners') sugar
25ml/1½ tbsp cold water
edible balls, to decorate

1 Preheat the oven to 180°C/350°F/Gas 4. Line two baking trays with baking parchment or silicone mats. For the cakes, whisk the butter and sugar until fluffy. Whisk in the egg.

2 In a separate bowl, sift the flour with the bicarbonate of soda, salt and ground spices, then stir in the orange rind. Fold half of the dry ingredients into the butter mixture. Mix in the buttermilk, then the rest of the dry ingredients. Fold in the dried fruit.

3 Using a piping or pastry bag fitted with a large plain nozzle, pipe 12 5cm/2in rounds of cake mixture 5cm/2in apart on each baking tray. Bake for 12–15 minutes, or until the cakes bounce back when gently pressed. Transfer to a wire rack to cool.

4 Using an oiled tablespoon, place some marshmallow creme filling on to the flat side of one cake and top with the flat side of another. Repeat to make 12 pies. Warm the brandy then drizzle on the tops of the pies. Leave to dry while you make the icing. Mix the royal icing sugar with the water to form a thick paste. Spread the icing roughly on the tops of the pies to create the texture of snow. Decorate with red and silver balls.

Energy 412kcal/1746kJ; Protein 4g; Carbohydrate 78g, of which sugars 59g; Fat 10g, of which saturates 6g; Cholesterol 44mg; Calcium 85mg; Fibre 1.7g; Sodium 350mg.

Christmas spice cakes

Mincemeat, brandy and freshly ground spices are the main ingredients in these delicious celebration cakes, which are ideal for those who love the rich spicy flavours of Christmas. The iced toppings will require a small snowflake or other Christmas themed cutter.

Makes 14

2 eggs
115g/4oz/½ cup golden caster (superfine) sugar
50ml/2fl oz/¼ cup double (heavy) cream
grated rind of 1 clementine
115g/4oz/⅓ cup mincemeat
115g/4oz/1 cup self-raising (self-rising) flour
2.5ml/½ tsp baking powder
5ml/1 tsp mixed (apple pie) spice
10ml/2 tsp brandy
50g/2oz/4 tbsp butter, melted

For the icing
350g/12oz/3 cups icing (confectioners') sugar, sifted
15ml/1 tbsp hot water
red food colouring

To decorate
175g/6oz sugarpaste
red paste food colouring (or use 115g/4oz pre-coloured red sugarpaste)

1 Preheat the oven to 180°C/350°F/ Gas 4. Line the cups of a bun tin or pan with paper cases.

2 Lightly beat the eggs with the sugar. Beat the cream into the egg mixture for about 1 minute, then add the grated clementine rind. Fold in the mincemeat. Sift in the flour, baking powder and mixed spice and fold in.

3 Finally add the brandy and the melted butter and stir to combine.

4 Half-fill the paper cases with the batter. Place in the centre of the oven and bake for 12–15 minutes until risen and golden. Test by lightly pressing the centre of the cakes with your fingertips; the sponge should spring back. Leave on a wire rack to cool.

5 To make the icing, mix the sugar with just enough hot water to make a soft icing. Tint one-third of it with the red food colour and spoon over four of the cakes. Ice the remaining cakes with the white icing.

6 Set aside one-third of the sugarpaste and colour the rest red. Roll both out and stamp out 10 red and 4 white snowflakes. Stick one on each cake before the icing sets.

Energy 272kcal/1153kJ; Protein 2g; Carbohydrate 56g, of which sugars 49.7g; Fat 6.1g, of which saturates 3.4g; Cholesterol 40mg; Calcium 43mg; Fibre 0.4g; Sodium 52mg.

Index

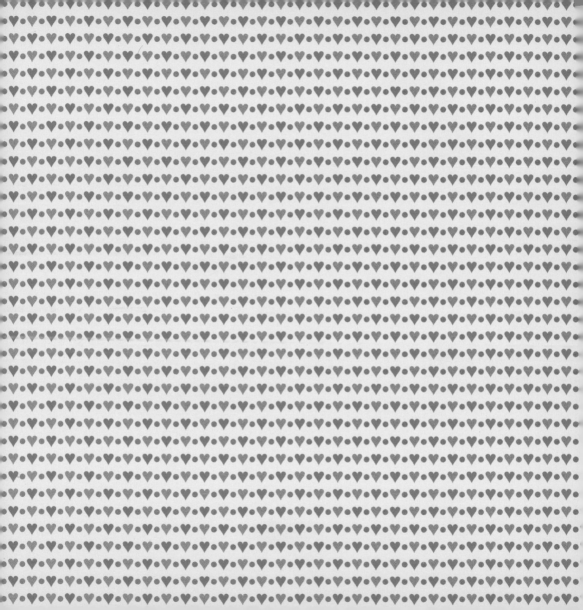